The
Unsha
TRUTH
Journey

GROWTH
GUIDES
for Adults

Perspective

*Experience
the World Through
God's Eyes*

JOSH McDOWELL
SEAN McDOWELL

HARVEST HOUSE PUBLISHERS
EUGENE, OREGON

Cover by Koechel Peterson & Associates, Inc., Minneapolis, Minnesota

Cover photo © Comstock / Thinkstock

THE UNSHAKABLE TRUTH is a trademark of The Hawkins Children's LLC. Harvest House Publishers, Inc., is the exclusive licensee of the federally registered trademark THE UNSHAKABLE TRUTH.

PERSPECTIVE—EXPERIENCE THE WORLD THROUGH GOD'S EYES
Course 10 of The Unshakable Truth® Journey
Copyright © 2012 by Josh McDowell Ministry and Sean McDowell
Published by Harvest House Publishers
Eugene, Oregon 97402
www.harvesthousepublishers.com

ISBN: 978-0-7369-4350-5 (pbk.)
ISBN: 978-0-7369-4352-9 (eBook)

Printed in the United States of America

12 13 14 15 16 17 18 19 20 / VP-SK / 10 9 8 7 6 5 4 3 2 1

CONTENTS

About the Authors

Authors Josh and Sean McDowell collaborated with their writer to bring you this Unshakable Truth Journey Growth Guide. The content is based upon Scripture and the McDowells' book *The Unshakable Truth*.

Over 50-plus years, **Josh McDowell** has spoken to more than 10 million people in 120 countries about the evidence for Christianity and the difference the Christian faith makes in the world. He has authored or coauthored more than 120 books (with more than 51 million copies in print), including such classics as *More Than a Carpenter* and *New Evidence That Demands a Verdict*.

Sean McDowell is an educator and a popular speaker at schools, churches, and conferences nationwide. He is author of *Ethix: Being Bold in a Whatever World*, coauthor of *Understanding Intelligent Design*, and general editor of *Apologetics for a New Generation* and *The Apologetics Study Bible for Students*. He is currently pursuing a PhD in apologetics and worldview studies. Sean's website, www.seanmcdowell.org, offers his blog, many articles and videos, and much additional curriculum.

About the Writer

Dave Bellis is a ministry consultant focusing on ministry planning and product development. He is a writer, producer, and product developer. He and his wife, Becky, have two grown children and live in northeastern Ohio.

Acknowledgments

We would like to thank the many people who brought creativity and insight to forming this course:

Terri Snead and David Ferguson of Great Commandment Network for their writing insights for the TruthTalk and Truth Encounter sections of this growth guide.

Terry Glaspey for his insights and guidance as he helped in the development of the Unshakable Truth Journey concept.

Paul Gossard for his skillful editing of this manuscript.

And finally, the entire team at Harvest House, who graciously endured the process with us.

Josh McDowell
Sean McDowell
Dave Bellis

WHAT IS THE UNSHAKABLE TRUTH JOURNEY ALL ABOUT?

You hear people talk about having a personal relationship with God and knowing Christ. But what does that really mean? Sure, they probably are saying they are a Christian and God has personally forgiven them of their sins. But is that all of what being a Christian really is—being a person forgiven by God?

We are here to say that being a follower of Christ is much, much more than that. Everything you are and what you are becoming as a person is wrapped up in it. When Jesus said he was "the way, the truth, and the life" (John 14:6) he was offering us a supernatural way to follow in his way, his truth, and his life. As we do, we begin to understand what we were meant to know and be and how we were meant to live. Actually, when we become a follower of Christ we begin to take on Jesus' view of the world and begin to think like and be motivated like and live like Christ. And that brings incredible joy and satisfaction to life.

So when we see life and relationships as Jesus sees them, we begin to get a clear picture of who we are and discover our true identity. We begin to realize why we are here and recognize our purpose and meaning in life. We begin to know where we are going and experience our destiny and mission in a life larger than ourselves. Being a Christian—a committed follower of Christ—unlocks our identity, purpose, and destiny in life. It is then that the natural process of spiritual reproduction takes place. That is when imparting the faith to our family and others around us becomes a reality. But what is involved in being that kind of a follower of Christ—a person who has joy and satisfaction in life and knows how to effectively impart the faith to the next generation?

The Unshakable Truth Journey gets to the core of what being a true follower of Christ means and what knowing Christ is all about. Together you and your group will begin a journey that will last a lifetime. It is a journey into what you as a follower of Christ are to believe biblically, how you process your beliefs into core values, and how you live them out in all your relationships. In fact, we will take the core truths of Christianity and break them down into a five-step process:

1. ***What truths do you as a Christian believe biblically?***

   In the first step you and your group will interact with what we as Christians believe about God, his Word, and so on.

2. ***Why do you believe those truths?***

   Sure, you can say you believe certain truths because they are biblical, but when you know *why* they are true it grounds you in your faith. Additionally, it gives you confidence to pass them on to others—especially your family.

3. ***How are these truths relevant to life?***

   In many respects truth isn't very meaningful until you see how it is relevant to your own life.

4. ***How do you live these truths out personally?***

   Knowing how the truth of Christianity is relevant is necessary, but what it leads to is understanding how that truth is to become a living reality in your own life. That's where the rubber meets the road, so to speak.

5. ***How do you, as a group, live these truths out before your community and world?***

   As Christians we are all to be "salt" and "light" to

the world around us. In this step you and your group will discover how to impact your own community with truth that is lived out corporately—as a body.

Be warned! The Unshakable Truth Journey isn't a program to study what Christianity is all about. Simply discovering what something is about has great limitations and ends up being of little value. Rather, this journey is about experiencing firsthand how God's truth is to be experienced in your life right now and, in fact, for the rest of your life. It's about knowing God's truth in a real, experiential way. The apostle John said, "It is by our actions that we know we are living in the truth" (1 John 3:19). You will be challenged repeatedly to increasingly know certain truths by experiencing them continually in your relationship with God and with those around you. It is then you will be able to pass on this ever-increasing faith journey to your family and friends.

There will be two specific exercises that appear throughout these courses. The first is entitled "Truth Encounter." This section is an invitation for you to stop and carefully reflect on the truth of each session. You'll be asked to encounter a truth of God as you relate personally with Jesus, as you live out the truth of God's Word with your small group, or as you relate personally with his people. Please don't rush past these Truth Encounters. They are designed to equip you in how to experience truth right in the room you're in!

The second exercise is an assignment for the week, called "TruthTalk." The TruthTalks are designed as conversation starters—ways to engage others in spiritual discussions. They will create opportunities for you to share what you've experienced in this course with others around you. This will help you communicate God's truth with others as you share vulnerably about your own Unshakable Truth Journey.

What you discover here is to last a lifetime and beyond. You will never finish in this life nor in the life to come. God's truths are designed to be enjoyed forever. You see, experiencing God's truth and knowing him will grow throughout eternity, and your love of him will expand to contain it. And that process begins in the here and now. Your relationship with God may have begun 5 months, 5 years, or 50 years ago—it doesn't matter. The truths explored in these courses are to be applied at every level of life. And what is so encouraging is that while these truths are eternally deep they can be embraced and experienced by even a young child. That is the beauty and mystery of God's truth!

This particular Unshakable Truth Journey is one of 12 different growth guides. All the growth guides are based upon Josh and Sean McDowell's book *The Unshakable Truth*, which is the companion book to this course. The book covers 12 core truths of the Christian faith.

The growth guide you have in your hand covers the truth about God's kingdom and how that gives us a biblical worldview.

These five sessions lay the foundation for how to gain this kind of worldview. Check out the other Unshakable Truth Journey courses in the back of this book.

Okay then, let our journey begin.

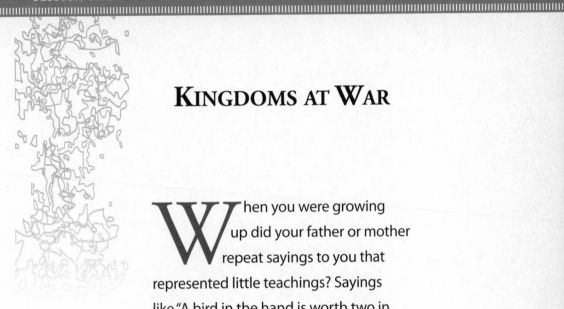

KINGDOMS AT WAR

When you were growing up did your father or mother repeat sayings to you that represented little teachings? Sayings like "A bird in the hand is worth two in the bush," "The road to hell is paved with good intentions," and so on. What were some of those sayings?

_____

_____

_____

_____

_____

_____

Most of those sayings represent a way of thinking and living, a philosophy of life, or what you might even call a worldview. Take a try at defining what _worldview_ means.

A _worldview_ means _____

_____

_____

_____

_____

Someone read the following.

A worldview is how we view all of life. It is what we assume to be true about the basic makeup of our world. A worldview is like a mental map of reality. We believe certain things about ourselves and God and life, and then we interpret our experiences through them. Everyone has a worldview, even though not everyone _realizes_ they have one.

Jesus' worldview—his view of life—is called a biblical worldview or kingdom-of-God worldview. Embracing Jesus' kingdom worldview means understanding and living life from God's perspective. It means understanding what we were meant to know and be and how we were meant to live. His worldview works because it explains the truth about God and about us. That is what Jesus and the whole of Scripture does—it gives us the truth about life, and the power to live according to the kingdom of God.

OUR GROUP OBJECTIVE

To gain a greater understanding of how two opposing worldviews—the kingdom of this world and the kingdom of heaven—affect every aspect of our lives and how to identify with Jesus' kingdom worldview.

Someone read John 18:33-37.

What did Jesus mean that his kingdom is not of this world? He created this world didn't he; then why isn't this world his kingdom? Discuss.

_____

_____

_____

_____

_____

_____

Someone read 1 John 5:19 and Ephesians 6:10-12.

What do these passages mean when they say that this world is under Satan's power and control and that our battle isn't with human beings? Aren't we supposed to help make our country a Christian nation?

_____

_____

_____

_____

_____

Someone read the following.

Jesus' kingdom idea was not about toppling the Roman Empire. His opposition wasn't the Romans or even the Jewish leaders. His opposition was Lucifer, his archenemy. You see, once Adam and Eve sinned it was Satan that moved in and made this present world his kingdom, the kingdom of darkness. So Jesus wasn't focused on human governments; he was focused on Satan's world order. Jesus came to earth to reclaim his lost creation and re-establish a circle of relationship between the Godhead (Father, Son, and Holy Spirit) and his human creation. The kingdom of God was to be a perfect relational order in which God's children loved and worshipped him, and together they would share in all the goodness and glory of his vast domain.

But sin destroyed the relationship between God and humans. Before the kingdom of this world could become the eternal kingdom of God, Satan gained control. In effect, Satan snatched the kingdom of this world away from God's children. Two kingdoms now exist—the kingdom of this world, with Satan as its king, and the kingdom of heaven with God as its King. That means that we are presently in the midst of a mighty conflict between two kingdoms warring against each other.

So the conflict isn't really political in nature as some people assume. The struggle isn't even a cultural one. The primary enemy isn't wicked people or evil regimes of this world. The war is between God and his ways and Satan and his ways.

What God did when he entered human history 2000 years ago was to put Satan on notice that the kingdom of this world was going to be rescued and conquered by the kingdom of heaven. Jesus saw this world as a stolen kingdom temporarily under the control of an enemy whose rule would one day come to an end. As C.S. Lewis put it, Christians on the earth live in "enemy-occupied territory."* But their loyalty is to their commander, Jesus, who is the leader of a spiritual resistance movement to free them from the rule of the usurper.

---

* C.S. Lewis, *Mere Christianity* (New York, NY: Macmillan, 1943), 36.

Differing Worldviews

How different does the kingdom of heaven operate than the kingdom of this world?

Someone read Matthew 5:38-42.

According to this passage:

The kingdom of this world says what about getting even?

_____

_____

_____

_____

_____

The kingdom of heaven says what about being persecuted?

_____

_____

_____

_____

_____

Someone read Matthew 6:31-33 and Matthew 19:29-30.

According to this passage:

The kingdom of this world says the important things in life are…

_____

_____

_____

_____

_____

The kingdom of heaven says the important things in life are…

_____

_____

_____

_____

_____

Someone read Matthew 5:21-22.

According to this passage:

The kingdom of this world defines murder as what?

_____

_____

_____

_____

The kingdom of heaven says you have committed murder in your heart when…

_____

_____

_____

_____

What are some other areas that contrast how the kingdom of this world and of heaven operate?

Kingdom of this world: _____

_____

_____

_____

_____

_____

Kingdom of heaven: _____

_____

_____

_____

_____

_____

Someone read the following from chapter 40 of *The Unshakable Truth.*

> This kingdom worldview—the Way of Jesus—
> may be spiritual in nature, but it affects every area
> of life. Jesus' worldview unlocks a very specific way
> of life, a way of knowing what is really true, a pic-
> ture of being what God meant us to be, and the

power to live that out based on our relationship with God. When we see and live by God's spiritual worldview, it combats darkness, injustice, and evil within the world. And that in turn brings resolution to the physical, economic, social, moral, ethical, and environmental problems of life. In fact, as we indicated earlier, God's new world order, which Jesus spiritually imparts to his followers today, will someday be a permanent and all-pervasive world order established in a new heaven and a new earth where there is no more sin, pain, sorrow, or death. But until the final and permanent kingdom of heaven envelops the kingdom of earth, we are to be his witnesses, the combatants against the spirit of darkness, and the messengers of Jesus' worldview, which is to be lived out for all to see.

Therefore:

> **We believe the truth that Jesus' kingdom-of-God life and message form our biblical worldview. It is this biblical worldview that not only provides us an accurate view of God, human history, life, relationships, death, and the world to come, but also a supernatural way to be and live in this present world.**

Truth Encounter

Someone read:

The kingdom of heaven isn't a permanent world order yet and the kingdom of this world is very pervasive. But that doesn't mean we are defenseless to protect our children, loved ones, and our own lives from Satan's plans. God has granted his children authority over the power of evil. And we can declare in Christ's name that the enemy has no authority over us or our loved ones.

Someone read Matthew 18:18-20.

Identify people or circumstances that you want protected from the enemy's power and plans. Then share that with the group.

_____

_____

_____

_____

_____

_____

_____

_____

_____

Take time as a group to pray over these people and situations. Declare in Jesus' name that the enemy has no authority here. Commit each person and situation into God's hands.

_____

_____

_____

_____

_____

_____

_____

Someone read Colossians 3:16-17.

Share your confidence and faith in God with each other. Sing songs together with hearts of thanks.

TruthTalk—An Assignment of the Week

Take time this week to share with your family or friend what you've been learning and how you have prayed a prayer of protection around them. Consider saying something like:

"Jesus answered, 'I am not an earthly king. If I were, my followers would have fought when I was arrested by the Jewish leaders. But my Kingdom is not of this world.'"… Jesus' kingdom idea was not about toppling the Roman Empire. His opposition wasn't the Romans or even the Jewish leaders. His opposition was Lucifer, his archenemy.

1 "In my group meeting this week we have been learning about the kingdom of heaven and the kingdom of this world. Here is some of what I've discovered:

_____

_____

_____."

2 "God has laid you on my heart and I've been praying that…

_____

_____

_____."

3 "I have been praying for you and want you to be protected from certain things. Lately I've been learning to trust God and praying that a hedge of protection will be built around you. I've been praying that…

_____

_____

_____."

Read chapter 41 of *The Unshakable Truth* book this week.

Close in Prayer

THE CORE CHARACTERISTIC OF JESUS' WORLDVIEW

Review: How did your TruthTalk assignment go this past week? What was the response?

_____

_____

_____

_____

_____

_____

Think back and identify one or two people who had a significant and positive impact on your life. Who was that person and how was it that you were impacted for good?

_____

_____

_____

_____

_____

_____

If you were to characterize the one quality that person who impacted you showed, what would that be?

_____

_____

_____

_____

_____

Jesus displayed many qualities. But one stands out that makes up the core of his worldview.

Various ones in your group read the following passages and identify the key quality of Jesus in each situation.

Matthew 9:36—The people's problems were great and Jesus was

_____

_____

_____

Matthew 14:13-14—The crowds followed Jesus and wanted to be healed and Jesus was _____

_____

_____

Matthew 15:32—The people hadn't eaten for some time and Jesus was _____

_____

_____

Matthew 20:34—Two blind men cried out to Jesus to heal them and Jesus was _____

_____

_____

Someone read 1 Peter 5:7.

What characterizes God's heart?

_____

The expression used most often to describe Jesus' heart was that he was "moved with compassion." God cares, and it is that caring heart of love that is at the core of Jesus' worldview.

OUR GROUP OBJECTIVE

To discover how the core characteristic of Jesus' worldview can be ours and how it impacts our relationships.

Someone read the following.

God cared enough that he "gave his only Son, so that everyone who believes in him will not perish but have eternal life" (John 3:16). Jesus cared enough that he was moved with compassion and continually reached out to people at the point of their need.

Someone read Matthew 7:12 and 1 Corinthians 13:4-5.

God has a caring heart of love. Yet what is the distinctive quality of this caring heart?

God's loving heart of care puts who first? _____.

And when we allow the Holy Spirit to live his loving heart of care through us, he produces what? (Read Galatians 5:22-23.)

_____

_____

_____

_____

Based on the various Scripture verses above, you have no doubt defined the characteristic of Jesus' kingdom worldview. Now define the core worldview characteristic of the kingdom of this world dominated by Satan.

Someone read Galatians 5:13-15,19-21.

The core worldview characteristic of the kingdom of this world puts who first? _____

_____.

Based on Galatians 5:19-21, what results from following this worldview?

_____

_____

_____

_____

Someone read the following. This is drawn from chapter 41 of *The Unshakable Truth* book.

> Some critics have characterized Christianity as an evil emperor imposing its will on the masses and threatening to suppress the free expressions of humanity. Although there are those past and present who, under the banner of Christianity, have waged war, enslaved people, and brought disgrace on the name of Christ, this is only a small, sad corner of the whole picture. It can be demonstrated that it is Jesus' kingdom worldview that has fostered more good and provided more positive contributions to society than any other force in history. If we were to highlight just a few of the positive influences of a biblical worldview they would include
>
> - the high value for human life
> - care for the sick in creating hospitals
> - literacy and education for the masses
> - abolition of slavery in the Western world

- the elevation of women

- high standards of justice and civil liberties

- benevolence and charity work

- development of art and music

- the motivation and basis for modern science

Atheists and other detractors of Christianity fail to point out that it is the human propensity to be self-centered that has brought such misery and suffering upon the masses. Christianity is actually the antidote to this propensity, for it is the message and power of Christ that addresses the core problem of self-centeredness.

Greed, corruption, abuse of power, and a basic disregard for others all spring from self-centeredness. Left unchecked, human nature will always revert to self-serving ways that seek to gain at another's expense. On the opposite side of the equation, making the interest and care of others as important as your own creates goodwill and harmony and meets human need.

At its core Jesus' biblical worldview represents a focus on caring for the interests of others. "In humility," Paul said, "consider others better than yourselves. Each of you should look not only to your own interests, but also to the interests of

others" (Philippians 2:3-4 NIV). This unselfish
compassion toward others was a radical message
when Jesus preached and lived it, and it still is now.

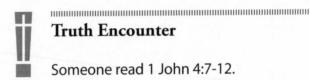

Truth Encounter

Someone read 1 John 4:7-12.

Jesus' other-centered worldview: *sacrificing one's own desires, needs, and interests in order to give to another, trusting that one's own desires, needs, and interests will be met in due time.*

Based on 1 John 4, what direct benefits have you received from God as a result of his other-centered focus toward you? How have you benefited from his love?

_____

_____

_____

_____

_____

_____

There are relational benefits to a person receiving other-centered love. When your spouse, children, parents, or friends sacrifice their own desires, needs, or interests to give to you, what does it do for you and in you? For example, you might say you feel appreciated, accepted, or cared for. Write below what additional benefits you receive.

_____

_____

_____

_____

_____

_____

_____

Think of a specific time when your spouse, parents, or close friend has shown you other-centered love. Now turn to your partner and share how you felt when he or she demonstrated that kind of love. For example, use your list above and say, "When you give unselfishly to me you make me feel (what?)"

_____

_____

_____

_____

_____

Now share with your group what you expressed to your partner.

There are also relational benefits for giving this other-centered love to others. When you give of yourself unselfishly you may experience joy, closeness, satisfaction, and so on. Write below

what additional benefits you receive when you give unselfishly
of yourself to your spouse, children, or friends.

_____

_____

_____

_____

_____

_____

Think of a specific time when you gave unselfishly of yourself
to your spouse, child, or close friend. Now turn to your partner
and share the benefits you received when you gave to him or
her unselfishly. For example, use your list above and say, "When
I give unselfishly to you I experience (what?)"

_____

_____

_____

_____

_____

_____

Now share with your group what you expressed with your partner.

The Solution to Self-Centeredness

Someone read 1 John 4:16-17.

Based on these verses, how do we overcome self-centeredness in order to love unselfishly?

_____

_____

_____

_____

_____

Someone read the following.

> If your answer is "to live in God and allow God to live in us," you would be correct. And allowing God to fill us with his love is critical. However, we unleash his unselfish love in our lives through a simple and sometimes difficult step. Our self-centered nature wants to take because we often fear that we won't get what we want or need. In other words, if we only look out for another's interest who is going to look out for ours? At the root of self-centeredness there is a lack of trust. The apostle John said, "We know how much God loves us, and we have put our trust in him" (1 John 4:16).

King David slept with another man's wife. He selfishly and lust-
fully took what didn't belong to him. He sinned against Bath-
sheba and certainly against her husband, Uriah. But was God
personally offended? Why? Someone read Psalm 51:4 and
2 Samuel 12:7-9.

_____

_____

_____

_____

_____

_____

Someone read the following:

> God says he is the one who satisfies every need
> there is (Acts 17:25). When we act on our self-
> centered tendencies we in effect say to God, "I
> don't really trust you to give me what I need when
> I need it." This is what King David said to God
> when he took selfishly. God told him that he had
> given him his house and his wives and the king-
> dom, and then said, "If that had not been enough,
> I would have given you much, much more"
> (2 Samuel 12:8). But David "despised [counted
> worthless] the word of the LORD" (verse 8).

Would it provide a deterrent for you when you are about to

act selfishly to realize you are hurting Jesus by saying in effect, "I don't believe you will meet my needs so I'm going to meet them myself"? Why or why not? Discuss.

_____

_____

_____

_____

_____

_____

What impact might it have on your family or friends if, when you apologize to them for some selfish behavior, you also share how your lack of trust in God has offended him as well? Discuss.

_____

_____

_____

_____

_____

_____

King David prayed to his great provider God, to whom he said, "You satisfy me more than the richest of foods" (Psalm 63:5). Someone read David's prayer found in Psalm 63:1-8 slowly.

He is our all-sufficient God who meets all our needs in due time. Sing to him. Give prayers of thanks to him. Share with one another how you want to trust in him more to meet your needs in his timing.

_____

_____

_____

_____

_____

_____

Truth**Talk—An Assignment of the Week**

Take time this week to share insights from this week's session with a family member or a friend. Consider saying something like:

Early Christians rejected the cultural practice of allowing abandoned babies and orphaned children to die on the streets. Instead, they would literally pick

1 "This week in my small group we've been discussing how when we act in a self-centered way it hurts God because…

_____

_____

_____."

them up and adopt them into their own homes. What caused them to do this? It was the "moved with compassion" heart of the Lord being lived out in their lives. Early Christians believed that everyone—including the poor, the homeless, the handicapped, the sick—was made in the image of God and had infinite value, dignity, and worth.

2 "I wanted to share with you how sorry I am that I have at times hurt you with my selfishness. And it also hurts God because…

_____

_____

_____."

3 "You know you have shown me such kindness recently when you _____, and your unselfish attitude has made me feel (accepted, appreciated, and so on)

_____

_____

_____."

Read chapter 42 of *The Unshakable Truth* book.

|||||||||||||||||||||||||||||||||||||||||||||||||||||||||||||||||||||||||||||||||

Close in Prayer

WHY YOUR WORLDVIEW MATTERS

Review: How did your TruthTalk assignment go this week? What was the response?

_____

_____

_____

_____

_____

_____

How many decisions did you make this week? Take a guess.

_____

Life involves constant, continual decisions, hundreds and hundreds of decisions each week. Identify just a few of the things you have decided this week. For example, this week you decided what you would eat, when you would eat, where you would eat it, and so on. What else did you decide to do with your mind, eyes, thoughts, hands, feet, speech, relationships, and so on? (Just a few.)

_____

_____

_____

_____

_____

Every decision you make or your children make or anyone around you makes is based on certain things we all believe about God, ourselves, and all of life. Everything we think and do is filtered through our assumptions of how life works.

OUR GROUP OBJECTIVE

To determine the basis of a Christ-centered worldview and how to live that out in our relationships.

Much of our view of life and how it works has its roots in the answers to three simple questions. How we and the general population answer these three questions probably differs.

Answer the following set of questions from a kingdom-of-God

worldview, from a kingdom-of-this-world worldview, and then how you would answer.

1. *Origin*: How did we humans get here?

Kingdom-of-God answer: _____

_____

_____

_____

Kingdom-of-this-world answer: _____

_____

_____

_____

Your answer: _____

_____

_____

_____

What view are your children taught at school? _____

_____

2. *Predicament*: What went wrong—why are there such problems in the world?

Kingdom-of-God answer: _____

_____

_____

_____

Kingdom-of-this-world answer: _____

_____

_____

_____

Your answer: _____

_____

_____

What view are your children taught at school?_____

_____

3. _Resolution_: What is the answer to the human dilemma?

Kingdom-of-God answer: _____

_____

_____

_____

Kingdom-of-this-world answer: _____

_____

_____

_____

Your answer: _____

_____

_____

What view are your children taught at school? _____

Based on a view of life from a kingdom-of-this-world perspective, who or what must we put our trust or hope in to resolve any problem of life?

_____

_____

_____

Every day we encounter the nitty-gritty areas of life, like having enough groceries, paying the bills, getting our kids through school, keeping a job, and so on. Who or what do we tend to rely on most in these situations? Our own efforts, human-made systems, God, or what?

_____

_____

_____

_____

Someone read Matthew 6:25.

Jesus said to not worry or fret about everyday life and the needs we have. But how are we not to worry about these things? Doesn't it say somewhere that "God helps those who help themselves"? What is the solution to our worries?

_____

_____

_____

_____

_____

What is Jesus' solution to our everyday worries and concerns of life?

Someone read Matthew 6:31-33.

_____

_____

_____

_____

_____

Contrast these two worldviews of how the worries of the everyday problems of life are resolved. Discuss.

_____

_____

_____

_____

_____

_____

Someone read Acts 17:24-25 and Philippians 4:19.

What do these two Scripture passages teach us as to who supplies all our needs?

_____

_____

_____

Do you believe God supplies all our needs?

☐ Yes   ☐ No   ☐ Sometimes
☐ I want to believe it   ☐ I struggle at times really believing it

If you truly believe God supplies all your needs, what is that belief based on? Before you answer that question, answer these two:

"Do you believe your spouse or mother or father loves you?"

_____.

"What is that belief based upon?" _____

_____

_____

_____

_____

Now, what is your belief that God supplies all your needs based upon?

_____

_____

_____

_____

_____

Someone read the following.

Everything you believe and how you came to believe it comes out of a relationship with someone or something. Your belief that your spouse or parents love you is founded on your relationship with them. Even if you believe they don't love you, it is based upon a relationship that has solidified your belief.

Let's say, for example, you truly believe God supplies all your needs as you seek him and his kingdom first according to Philippians 4:19 and Matthew 6:31-33. That belief comes out of a relationship with a God who you trust cares for you. You have given all your worries and cares to God because "he cares about what happens to you" (1 Peter 5:7).

Your relationship with God has formed and solidified your belief that he is a provider God. And that belief has in turn shaped your values. Your values therefore would not be a materialistic value system. Rather than being self-reliant and depending on your own strength to build up treasures on earth you would depend upon God for your needs. Your belief in the value of spiritual things would then drive your actions (see diagram). You give rather than take. You are not stingy and money-grubbing. You are storing up treasures in heaven. And when the stock market drops you probably don't get ulcers.

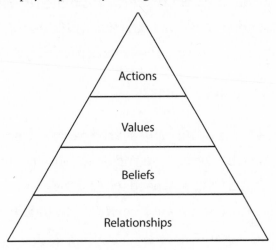

Discuss other examples of how everything we do is processed through this filter of relationships, beliefs, and values. Take, for example, an action like lying or cheating or stealing and identify the value system, the belief, and the relationship that reinforced or caused that belief.

_____

_____

_____

_____

_____

_____

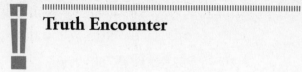

Truth Encounter

Living out a kingdom-of-God worldview is rooted in our biblical beliefs and founded upon our faith relationship with God, who has taken up residence in our lives through his Holy Spirit.

Someone read Hebrews 11:1-3.

The kingdom-of-this-world mind-set can easily influence us to believe more in what we can see and do for ourselves than in a God we can't see. Has this "I need to see it to believe it" mind-set influenced you in some way? How? Discuss together.

_____

_____

_____

_____

_____

Someone read Hebrews 11:13 and Hebrews 12:1-2.

Our biblical worldview is based upon a trusting relationship in a God who cares for us on a very deep level. The writer of Hebrews urges us to "strip off" that weight (sin) that hinders us so we can keep our eyes fixed on Jesus.

What are some of those weights or hindrances that keep you from deepening your trust and reliance upon God? Prayerfully write out what those are before God. These are things that you may do to feel secure, accepted, approved of, and so on.

_____

_____

_____

_____

_____

_____

Transparently share with the group some of those things that tend to hinder your deepened dependence upon God.

What does keeping your eyes fixed on Jesus (Hebrews 12:2) look like in your life? In other words, what attitudes or actions keep your heart and mind fixed on Jesus' way of giving unselfishly to others? Write these things out below.

_____

_____

_____

_____

_____

_____

Share what you have written with those in the group.

Someone prayerfully read Psalm 119:1-16.

Pray together as a group and ask God to teach you his ways. Thank him. Praise him. Sing songs of praise.

_____

_____

_____

_____

_____

_____

TruthTalk—An Assignment of the Week

Take time this week to share insights from this week's session with a family member or a friend. Consider saying something like:

Dr. James Sire… states that a world-view is "a commitment, a fundamental orientation of the heart, that can be expressed as a story or in a set of presuppositions (assumptions

1 "I've been learning in my small group what makes up a world-view—how we see ourselves and all of life. We answered three questions to discover what forms our views of life. I'd like to ask you those questions. Would that be okay?" (Questions: 1. How did

which may be true, partially true or utterly false) which we hold (consciously or subconsciously, consistently or inconsistently) about the basic constitution of reality, and that provides the foundation on which we live and move and have our being."*

we as humans get here? 2. What went wrong—why are there such problems in the world? 3. What is the answer to the problems of us humans?)

"_____

_____

_____."

2 "I'd like to share with you a little of what I'm learning in my small group about where our acting out comes from." (Share the relationship, belief, value process that leads to actions).

"_____

_____

_____."

3 "I've been personally discovering that a lot of my worries about material things are solved by embracing Jesus' worldview. Jesus said not to worry about those things

---

* James W. Sire, *The Universe Next Door* (Downers Grove, IL: InterVarsity, 2009), 20.

but to trust in a God who takes care of us. Here's how I'm working on that:

_____

_____

_____."

Read chapter 43 of *The Unshakable Truth* book.

||||||||||||||||||||||||||||||||||||||||||||||||||||||||||||||||||||||||||||||||||||||||||||||||||||||

Close in Prayer

SEE LIFE AS GOD SEES IT

Review: How did your TruthTalk assignment go this week? What was the response?

_____

_____

_____

_____

_____

_____

Throughout this course we have interacted about the Trinity, the Holy Spirit, and a Christ-centered worldview. Has it surprised you how much influence the kingdom of this world has on us, our friends in church, and our children? How so?

_____

_____

_____

_____

_____

Someone read John 17:13-17 and 21-22.

Jesus prayed for his disciples and he has prayed for us that we might not be of this world. What is it that will keep us from being part of the kingdom of this world?

_____

_____

_____

_____

_____

OUR GROUP OBJECTIVE

To gain a greater understanding of Jesus' view of life and how, by embracing his view as ours, we will find both wisdom and joy.

Someone read the following. (This is drawn from chapter 35 of *The Unshakable Truth* book.)

Living in this world but not being a part of it does

not happen naturally. We are surrounded by a
world that clamors for our attention and attempts
to draw our hearts in its direction. It is a world of
busyness that compels us to cope with life in all its
difficulties and troubles. That is the world we see
with human eyes. Our task is to see yet another
world that is invisible to the natural man and
woman. It is the world through which Jesus sees
all of life. As we become one with him through the
power of the Holy Spirit we can see and live life as
he sees it. It is then that we become both wise and
full of joy and peace.

For the rest of this session let's take just one of the twelve
truths from *The Unshakable Truth* book and engage in a "Truth
Encounter." We will identify the truth, our relationship with
the truth-giver, and what we believe about that truth. Then
together as a group, you will identify the values you have
formed as a result of your beliefs and how that plays out in your
attitudes and actions. This exercise is designed to help you see
and live life as Jesus sees it.

Your Relationship

- Who created the world and all that exists? _____

- Who died for you that you might live? _____

- Who rose again and sits at God's right hand praying and interceding for you? _____

- Who enters your life to tell you that you are God's child (Romans 8:16), makes you intimate with God (John 17:21-23), and is conforming you to Christ's image (2 Corinthians 3:18)?

  _____

- Who do you love and worship? (Exodus 34:14 and Matthew 22:37) _____

What a relationship! God is now your loving Father. God's Son, Jesus, loved you so much he died to save you from an eternity without God and redeem you back to being a son or daughter of God. God the Holy Spirit has entered your life to make your intimate relationship with God a living reality. That relationship forms the basis for many of your beliefs, your values, and your attitudes and actions.

Your Beliefs

- Our relational God epitomizes and defines the very meaning of _____, for Scripture says, "God is _____" (1 John 4:16).

- God is a Trinity in the persons of God the _____, God the _____, and God the _____, who are three persons with infinite love for each other in perfect relationship.

- We have been created in God's image and as such we are to experience the relational intimacy of love with _____ and with one _____.

- The love of the triune Godhead provides us a model of love and oneness in perfect unity with one another, and it additionally explains the "reason a man will leave his father and mother and be united to his _____, and they will become _____" (Genesis 2:24 NIV).

- The Holy Spirit enters our lives, and as we make him at _____ in our hearts he will empower us to live a life pleasing to God.

Our relationship with God forms our beliefs about a relational God who loves us unselfishly, about the meaning of a love relationship, and about how he empowers us to live out his kind of relationship.

||||||||||||||||||||||||||||||||||||||||||||||||||||||||||||||||||||||||||||||||||||||||||||||||

Your Values

Based on your beliefs, would you then value human life? Why?

_____

_____

_____

_____

_____

Would you value the physical and emotional needs of humans?
Why?

_____

_____

_____

_____

Would you value Planet Earth? Why?

_____

_____

_____

_____

Based on your beliefs, would you value the relational uniting of
a man and a woman in marriage? Why?

_____

_____

_____

_____

Would you value giving of yourself, even sacrificially, to produce increasing relational intimacy with your spouse? Why?

_____

_____

_____

_____

_____

Would you value the marriage relationship enough to want it to last five years, ten years, or a lifetime? Why?

_____

_____

_____

_____

_____

Based on your beliefs, would you value worship of God and spending time to know how to make him more and more at home in your heart? Why?

_____

_____

_____

_____

_____

Truth Encounter:

Your Attitudes and Actions

Based on your relationship with God and who he is, your beliefs about him, and your values, how then are you to live?

What are your attitudes and actions regarding human life? What is your attitude toward murder, war, unborn life, the dignity of life, and so on? Discuss how your values affect your actions in these areas.

_____

_____

_____

_____

What are your attitudes and actions regarding the physical and emotional needs of others? What is your attitude toward putting things in the body that harm it, engaging in immoral acts that contract disease, caring for the sick, defending the rights of others, social justice, protecting the innocent, and so on? Discuss how your values affect your actions in these areas.

_____

_____

_____

_____

What are your attitudes and actions regarding Planet Earth? What is your attitude toward depleting the planet of its resources without regard to replenishing it, animal life, pollution, and so on? Discuss how your values affect your actions in these areas.

_____

_____

_____

_____

_____

What are your attitudes and actions regarding the relationship of marriage? What is your attitude regarding same-sex marriage, a commitment to give sacrificially to increase relational intimacy in marriage, the permanency of marriage, adultery, divorce, and so on? Discuss how your values affect your actions in these areas.

_____

_____

_____

_____

_____

What are your attitudes and actions regarding your worship of God and developing intimacy with Jesus? What is your attitude regarding your devotion to God, how much you put your trust in him to supply your needs, unselfishly giving to him and others, the amount of time you spend getting to know him, and so on? Discuss how your values affect your actions in these areas.

_____

_____

_____

_____

_____

_____

|||||||||||||||||||||||||||||||||||||||||||||||||||||||||||||||||||||||||||||||||||||||||||||||||

Summary Questions

What often hinders us from living out what we say we believe? Discuss together and identify some reasons or hindrances that keep us from seeing our beliefs transform our values, which results in corresponding behavior.

_____

_____

_____

_____

_____

Our relationship is the foundation to our attitudes and actions. The deeper our relationship with God, the more that relationship will be reflected in our behavior. King David understood that and therefore had a deep thirst to know God. Psalm 145 is a passage of praising God for who he is and demonstrating how his relationship touches us at the point of our need.

Someone prayerfully read Psalm 145:8-21. Take time to thank God for his loving relationship and ask him to help you reflect his relationship with you through your beliefs, values, and actions. Sing songs of praise.

_____

_____

_____

_____

_____

_____

TruthTalk—An Assignment of the Week

Take time this week to share insights from this week's session with a family member or a friend. Consider saying something like:

Your biblical worldview gives you a clear sense of your identity, purpose, and destiny in life. As God empowers you to live out your worldview, he completes you, gives you a sense of meaning, and provides you an expectant hope of an eternal future. No other worldview provides so much joy. No other worldview provides such overwhelming evidence that it is true.

1 "I've been having some interesting discussions this week in my small group about how our relationship with God affects every aspect of our lives and the world around us. Here's an interesting question: 'How does our belief in God affect our attitude about starving children (or war in the Middle East, or caring for the homeless, orphans, or the sick, and so on)?'

_____

_____

_____."

2 "Do you know how our deepened relationship with God makes a huge difference in how we treat

No other worldview provides for such a glorious future.

others? Let me share with you what I've been learning:

_____

_____

_____."

Review chapter 43 of *The Unshakable Truth* book this week.

Close in Prayer

LIVING OUT YOUR WORLDVIEW WITHIN YOUR COMMUNITY

Review: How did your TruthTalk assignment go this week? What was the response with those you shared?

_____

_____

_____

_____

_____

_____

Someone read James 1:27 and James 2:14-17.

Based on your biblical worldview, what is the relationship between worshipping God and caring for orphans, widows, and those in need of food and clothing?

_____

_____

_____

_____

_____

_____

Someone read Psalm 112:9.

King David said that those who fear the Lord give generously to those in need. What happens to those good deeds?

_____

_____

_____

_____

Someone read the following.

When you as a group do good based on your biblical world-view, God is glorified and he is pleased to give you influence and honor in the community.

OUR GROUP OBJECTIVE

To plan a group activity that involves doing deeds for others in your community to bring honor to God.

In this session you as a group are to brainstorm about an effort to reach out to people in the community to meet some emotional, relational, or physical needs in their lives. This could be to orphans, widows, those who are hungry, in need of clothing, and so on.

Brainstorm: _____

_____

_____

_____

_____

_____

Take the time here to plan your project by using the following steps:

Identify your activity: _____

_____

_____

_____

Set the date and time for your activity: _____

_____

_____

_____

Determine what is needed to execute your activity: _____

_____

_____

_____

Assign responsibilities and tasks for who will be doing what:

_____

_____

_____

Have someone in your group track and record what is being done. This is to record the results of your efforts:

_____

_____

_____

Bring every aspect of your activity before the Lord.

Someone read Matthew 6:1-2.

As you close in prayer tell God you want him to get the praise and honor for your ministry to those in need.

Assignment of the Week

Execute your activity.

Close in Prayer

Take the Complete Unshakable Truth® Journey!

The Unshakable Truth Journey gets to the heart of what being a true follower of Christ means and what knowing him is all about. Each five-session course is based on one of 12 core truths of the Christian faith presented in Josh and Sean McDowell's book *The Unshakable Truth*®.

The Unshakable Truth Journey is uniquely positioned for today's culture because it 1) highlights how Christianity's beliefs affect relationships, 2) promotes a relational, group context in which Christians can experience the teaching in depth, and 3) shows believers how they can live out Christianity's central truths before their community and world.

More than just a program, The Unshakable Truth Journey is a tool for long-term change and transformation!

CREATED—EXPERIENCE YOUR UNIQUE PURPOSE is devoted to the truth that God is—he exists, and he created human beings for a reason. It lays a foundation for who people are because they're God's creation, who God designed them to be, and how they can live a life of fulfillment.

INSPIRED—EXPERIENCE THE POWER OF GOD'S WORD explores the truth that God has spoken and revealed himself to humanity within the Bible. Further, he gave us his Word for a very clear purpose—to provide for us and protect us.

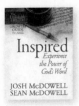

BROKEN—EXPERIENCE VICTORY OVER SIN examines the truth about humankind's brokenness because of original sin, humankind's ongoing problem with sin, and how instead to make right choices in life.

ACCEPTED—EXPERIENCE GOD'S UNCONDITIONAL LOVE opens up the truth about God's redemption plan. The truth that God became human establishes his unconditional acceptance of us, which defines our worth. God values us in spite of our sin. This is the basis on which we gain a high sense of worth.

Sacrifice—Experience a Deeper Way to Love digs into the truth about Christ's atonement. The truth that Christ had to die to purchase our salvation shows the true meaning of love—and how God can bring us into a right relationship with him in spite of our sin.

Forgiven—Experience the Surprising Grace of God explores the truth about the power of God's grace. The truth that God can offer us forgiveness in spite of our sin helps us understand how we actually obtain a relationship with him.

Growing—Experience the Dynamic Path to Transformation speaks to the truth about our transformed life in Christ. The truth about our transformed life in Christ defines who we are in this world and shows how we can know our purpose in life.

Resurrected—Experience Freedom from the Fear of Death focuses on the truth about Christ's resurrection. The truth that Christ rose from the grave and that his resurrection is a historical event assures us of eternal life and overcomes any fear of dying.

Empowered—Experience Living in the Power of the Spirit covers the truth about the Trinity. The truth that God is three in one and defines how relationships work through the Holy Spirit lays the foundation for how we can experience the power of the Spirit.

Perspective—Experience the World Through God's Eyes examines the truth about God's kingdom and how it defines a biblical worldview. These sessions show how to gain a biblical worldview.

Community—Experience Jesus Alive in His People opens up the truth about the church. The truth about Christ's body—the church—provides us with our mission in life and shows us how to experience true community.

Restored—Experience the Joy of Your Destiny is devoted to the truth about the return of Christ. The truth that Jesus is coming back helps us grasp our destiny in life and gain an eternal perspective on life and death.

The Unshakable Truth Journey
Perspective Growth Guide Evaluation Form

1. How many on average participated in your group? _____

2. Did you read all or a portion of *The Unshakable Truth* book? _____

3. Did your group leader use visual illustrations during this course? _____

4. *Group leader:* Was your experience connecting to the web and viewing the video illustrations acceptable? Explain.

   _____

   _____

5. On a scale of 1 to 10 (10 being the highest) how would you rate:

   a) the quality and usefulness of the session content? _____
   b) the responsiveness and interaction of those in your group? _____

6. To what degree did this course deepen your practical understanding of the truths it covered?

   ❏ Little   ❏ Somewhat   ❏ Rather considerably

   Please give any comments you feel would be helpful to us.

   _____

   _____

   _____

   _____

Please mail to: Josh McDowell Evaluation
PO Box 4126
Copley, OH 44321

The Unshakable Truth® church and small group resource collections are part of a unique collaboration between Harvest House Publishers and the Great Commandment Network. The Great Commandment Network is an international network of denominational partners, churches, parachurch ministries and strategic ministry leaders who are committed to the development of ongoing Great Commandment ministries worldwide as they prioritize the powerful simplicity of loving God, loving others and making disciples.

Through accredited trainers, the Great Commandment Network equips churches for ongoing relational ministry utilizing resources from the GC² Experience collection.

The GC² Experience Vision

To provide process-driven resources for a lifelong journey of spiritual formation. Every resource includes intentional opportunities to live out life-changing content within the context of loving God, loving others, and making disciples (Matthew 22:37-40; 28:19-20).

The GC² Experience Process includes:

■ Experiential and transformative content. People are relationally transformed when they encounter Jesus, experience his Word, and engage in authentic community.

■ Opportunities to move through a journey of…

• Exploring Truth in the safety of relationship
• Embracing Truth in a personal way
• Experiencing Truth in everyday life
• Expressing Truth through my identity as a Christ-follower

"Most of us have attended too many meetings and have gone through too many courses, only to conclude: We're leaving unchanged, and the people in our lives can see that we're unchanged. It is time to trust God for something different…a movement of life-changing transformation!"

Dr. David Ferguson
The Great Commandment Network

**The Transforming Promise of
Great Commandment/Great Commission Living**
www.GC2experience.com

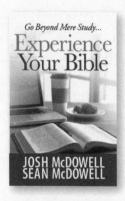

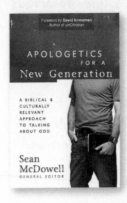

Apologetics for a New Generation
A Biblical and Culturally Relevant Approach to Talking About God
Sean McDowell

Sean McDowell and his first-rate team of contributors show how you can help members of the new generation plant their feet firmly on the truth. Find out how you can walk them through the process of…

- formulating a biblical worldview and applying scriptural principles to everyday issues

- articulating their questions and addressing their doubts in a safe environment

- becoming confident in their faith and effective in their witness

The truth never gets old, but people need to hear it in fresh, new ways. Find out how you can effectively share the answers to life's big questions with a new generation.

The Awesome Book of Bible Answers for Kids
Josh McDowell and Kevin Johnson

These concise, welcoming answers include key Bible verses and explorations of topics that matter most to kids ages 8 to 12: God's love; right and wrong; Jesus, God's Word; different beliefs and religions; and others. Josh and Kevin look at questions like…

- How do I know God wants to be my friend?

- Are parts of the Bible make-believe, or is everything true?

- Why do some Christians not act like Christians?

- Can God make bad things turn out okay?

The next time a child in your life asks a good question, this practical and engaging volume will give you helpful tips and conversation ideas.

The Amazing Bible Adventure for Kids
Finding the Awesome Truth in God's Word
Josh McDowell and Kevin Johnson

Josh McDowell, author of *The Unshakable Truth*® and many other resources, joins pastor and bestselling author Kevin Johnson to map out a quest for children ages 7 to 11—a quest that will lead them to the discovery that God is truth, and that real happiness comes from knowing him as he is revealed in his Word. With fun facts, questions, and laugh-out-loud stories, McDowell and Johnson simplify the tough concepts and bring boys and girls to the most amazing treasure of all!